American Watercolor Society

**AWS - 1891**

American Watercolor Society

**AWS - 1891**

ISBN/EAN: 9783337300128

Printed in Europe, USA, Canada, Australia, Japan

Cover: Foto ©Andreas Hilbeck / pixelio.de

More available books at **www.hansebooks.com**

# ILLUSTRATED CATALOGUE OF THE TWENTY-FOURTH ANNUAL EXHIBITION OF THE AMERICAN WATER COLOR SOCIETY.

HELD AT THE GALLERIES OF THE

## NATIONAL ACADEMY OF DESIGN,

COR. TWENTY-THIRD STREET & FOURTH AVE.

OPEN FROM FEBRUARY 2D TO FEBRUARY 28TH.

NEW YORK.

1891

Moss Engraving Co
New York.

# THE ILLUSTRATED CATALOGUE

PUBLISHED BY THE

## New York Etching Club

this year is the beginning of a new series. In it there are etchings never before published, by Messrs. Colman, Church, Platt, Lathrop and Chapman, and a Kurtz portrait of each etcher.

A preface treats of the popular demand and supply of etchings, describes briefly several methods of etching and engraving and speculates concerning the future of the art of etching in this country.

In succeeding publications each member of the Club will be represented. When the series is complete it will form a collection of examples of the etched work of all of the members of the Club, with portraits of each, and short essays pertinent to the art and its interests.

The edition is a very small one, being limited to five hundred copies at one dollar each. For sale at the desk. Orders should be sent to

ALEXANDER SCHILLING,
*Secretary.*
49 WEST 22D STREET.

No. 359.   Eleanor—Frederick Dielman.

OFFICERS

OF THE

# AMERICAN WATER COLOR SOCIETY.

## 1890-91.

### BOARD OF CONTROL.

J. G. Brown, *President*.
C. Harry Eaton, *Secretary*.
J. Symington, *Treasurer*.

Henry Farrer.                    Henry P. Smith.
R. M. Shurtleff.                 H. W. Ranger.

### JURY OF ADMISSIONS.

J. G. Brown.                     C. Harry Eaton.
J. Symington.                    H. W. Ranger.
Henry Farrer.                    R. M. Shurtleff.
Henry P. Smith.                  F. S. Church.
J. Francis Murphy.      ~        Hamilton Hamilton.

### HANGING COMMITTEE.          ### CATALOGUE COMMITTEE.
F. S. Church.                    T. de Thulstrup.
J. Francis Murphy.               Wm. H. Lippincott.
Hamilton Hamilton.               C. Harry Eaton.

### COMMITTEE ON DECORATIONS.
J. C. Nicoll.
F. C. Jones.
James D. Smillie.

# NOTICES.

ILLUSTRATIONS MARKED WITH A (✱) ARE FROM DRAWINGS MADE
BY THE ARTISTS.

FOR INFORMATION IN REGARD TO WORKS FOR SALE, INQUIRE OF
MR. GEO. H. GALT, AT THE DESK IN THE GALLERY.

ALL PAYMENTS SHOULD BE MADE BEFORE THE CLOSE OF THE
EXHIBITION, TO THE ORDER OF JAMES SYMINGTON, TREAS.

PRICES INCLUDE FRAMES.

# TO EXHIBITORS.

THE WM. T. EVANS PRIZE OF THREE HUNDRED DOLLARS FOR
THE MOST MERITORIOUS PICTURE IN THE EXHIBITION
WILL BE AWARDED BY VOTE OF THE SOCIETY
AS SOON AS PRACTICABLE AFTER THE
OPENING OF THE EXHIBITION.

# NORTH GALLERY.

| NO. | SUBJECT. | OWNER OR PRICE. | ARTIST. |
|---|---|---|---|
| 1 | A Pantry Window, | $125.00 | Frederick Dielman. |
| 2 | Hackensack Meadows Overflowed, | 50.00 | C. Harry Eaton. |
| 3 | The Pond of the Manor House, | 90.00 | John A. Frazer. |
| 4 | Harvest Field, Surrey, | 75.00 | Charles Parsons. |
| 5 | Late Twilight, Central Park, | 400.00 | J. C. Nicoll. |
| 6 | Last Leaves, November, | 175.00 | W. S. Bucklin. |
| 7 | King Birds Fighting Southern Kite, | 50.00 | Frederick Marschall. |
| 8 | Among the Rocks, | 100.00 | Francis C. Jones. |
| 9 | Amor Rex, | 150.00 | Albert Herter. |
| 10 | Katwijk Church, Holland, | Mr. H. H. Vail, | Will H. Drake. |
| 11 | A Cloud Study, Lake of Geneva, | 75.00 | J. Wells Champney. |
| 12 | Sunny November, | 30.00 | Chas. Eugene Moss. |

# NORTH GALLERY.

| NO. | SUBJECT. | OWNER OR PRICE. | ARTIST. |
|---|---|---|---|
| 13 | The Seine at Charenton, France, | $75.00 | George H. Bogert. |
| 14 | A Pastoral, | Mrs. Albert King, | Horatio Walker. |
| 15 | An Autumn Idyl, | 100.00 | Richard Newton, Jr. |
| 16 | A View in Eastern Pennsylvania, (Illustration.) | 40.00 | Wm. L. Sonntag. |
| 17 | Moonlight, Salt Meadows, | 45.00 | C. C. Benham. |
| 18 | Uplands, | 250.00 | Bruce Crane. |
| 19 | November Pastures, | 300.00 | J. A. S. Monks. |
| 20 | Landscape, | 40.00 | Edward L. Field. |
| 21 | On the Road to Conway, | 40.00 | Wm. L. Sonntag. |
| 22 | The League of Jonth, | 180.00 | Albert Herter. |
| 23 | A Weedy Place, | 35.00 | Mrs. J. Francis Murphy. |
| 24 | The Last Gleam, | 50.00 | De Lancey Gill. |
| 25 | A Bright Morning, | Mrs. A. | R. M. Shurtleff. |
| 26 | Twins, | 225.00 | Hugo Breul. |
| 27 | Moonrise, Cape May Point, | 60.00 | James Henry Moser. |
| 28 | Chums, | 250.00 | L. C. Earle. |
| 29 | In the Dunes, North Holland, | 125.00 | George Wharton Edwards. |
| 30 | Portrait, | E. V. Connett, | John A. MacDougall. |
| 31 | Rocky Pasture, Autumn, | 150.00 | W. Hamilton Gibson. |
| 32 | Winter, | 125.00 | H. Bolton Jones. |
| 33 | The Old Skipper, | 75.00 | Walter Satterlee. |
| 34 | After the Rain, | 100.00 | H. Bolton Jones. |
| 35 | The Tribute to King Minos, | 100.00 | Richard Newton, Jr. |
| 36 | Midwinter, | 75.00 | Walter L. Palmer. |
| 37 | Still Life, | 30.00 | J. N. Hutchins. |
| 38 | A Hothouse Flower, | 125.00 | Irving R. Wiles. |
| 39 | A Summer Idyl, (Illustration.) | 100.00 | Jos. Lauber. |
| 40 | A Family Group, | 35.00 | A. M. Curtis. |

6

No. 354   Mending Nets—Winslow Homer.

* No. 87.   A Summer Afternoon—Wm. T. Richards.

| NO. | SUBJECT. | OWNER OR PRICE. | ARTIST. |
|---|---|---|---|
| 41 | A Seine Boat, | $75.00 | Will S. Robinson. |
| 42 | A Scottish Solitude, | 350.00 | John A. Frazer. |
| 43 | May, | 135.00 | Wm. J. Whittemore. |
| 44 | Early Winter Morning, | 65.00 | Bruce Crane. |
| 45 | Mt. Sir Donald, Canadian Pacific Road, | 150.00 | Sam'l Colman. |
| 46 | Cloud Shadows, | 85.00 | Carleton T. Chapman. |
| 47 | Dutch Fishing Boat, (Illustration.) | Mr. H. H. Vail, | Will H. Drake. |
| 48 | Portia, | 125.00 | Jas. Symington. |
| 49 | Sunlight and Shadow, | 75.00 | Carleton Wiggins. |
| 50 | A Back Road, | 95.00 | James D. Smillie. |
| 51 | Sketch, | 15.00 | Miss Sophie M. Nichols. |
| 52 | The Census Enumerator— (An Indiscreet Question), | 750.00 | William T. Smedley. |
| 53 | Evening, | 175.00 | H. W. Ranger. |
| 54 | Gathering Driftwood, | 150.00 | Edward Moran. |
| 55 | Moonrise, | 175.00 | Richard Pauli. |
| 56 | Cloudy Day, October, | 200.00 | Henry Farrer. |
| 57 | Violets, | 20.00 | E. J. Holgate. |
| 58 | Dressing the House, | 125.00 | M. L. Stone. |
| 59 | The Latest Song, | 400.00 | J. G. Brown. |
| 60 | Roadscene, Devonshire, | 50.00 | Chas. Parsons. |
| 61 | Mamma's Favorite Song, | 350.00 | W. J. McCloskey. |
| 62 | The Lion of Belfort, (Illustration.) | 125.00 | C. E. Cookman. |
| 63 | Early Autumn in New Jersey, | 125.00 | C. Harry Eaton. |
| 64 | Still Water of the Croton, Mahopac, N. Y., | 225.00 | John A. Frazer. |
| 65 | Lady Maude, | 100.00 | Albert E. Sterner. |
| 66 | Misty Morning on Holford Moor, | 135.00 | Geo. H. McCord. |
| 67 | Day Dreams, | 75.00 | W. H. Holmes. |

# NORTH GALLERY.

| NO. | SUBJECT. | OWNER OR PRICE. | ARTIST. |
|---|---|---|---|
| 68 | A Hill Top, | $200.00 | J. Francis Murphy. |
| 69 | A Cossack, (Illustration.) | 250.00 | T. de Thulstrup. |
| 70 | October Afternoon, | 35.00 | C. Austin Needham. |
| 71 | Winter, Central Park, | 250.00 | D. W. Tryon. |
| 72 | Buying Herring, Coast of Maine, (Illustration.) | 200.00 | Carleton T. Chapman. |
| 73 | A Bit of Jersey, | 75.00 | E. J. Dressler. |
| 74 | " Puves," near Bristol, Eng. | | W. A. Sharp. |
| 75 | A Street in Gloucester, | 150.00 | Childe Hassam. |
| 76 | In the Garden, | 75.00 | Francis C. Jones. |
| 77 | Rijsburgh Church, Holland, | Mr. H. H. Vail, | Will H. Drake. |
| 78 | Elsa, | 40.00 | Amy Livingston Kellogg. |
| 79 | A Country Cousin, | 50.00 | Henry B. Snell. |
| 80 | South Transept, Santa Croce, | 55.00 | Miss A. M. Smart. |
| 81 | On the Sands, Manomet, | For sale, | Hamilton Hamilton. |
| 82 | A Nantucket Back Door, | 50.00 | Geo. M. Clark. |
| 83 | Winter Evening, Wainscot, L. I., | 150.00 | Sam'l Colman. |
| 84 | The Village Beauty, | 100.00 | Walter Satterlee. |
| 85 | Early Autumn, | 40.00 | A. Van Cleef Dodgshun. |
| 86 | Sunlight and Shadow, | 50.00 | Chas. A. Walker. |
| 87 | A Summer Afternoon, (Illustration.) | 500.00 | Wm. T. Richards. |
| 88 | Indian Beauties, | 100.00 | Agnes D. Abbatt. |
| 89 | Water Lilies, | | Agnes F. Northrup. |
| 90 | A Curricle Ride, 1790, | 350.00 | T. de Thulstrup. |
| 91 | Thistles, | 100.00 | Henry W. Parton. |
| 92 | The Close of Day, | 18.00 | Carrie Stow Wait. |
| 93 | Old Gate, Montmorency, France, | 50.00 | Geo. M. Clark. |
| 94 | Fiction, | 40.00 | George E. Graves. |

* No. 466.  Concarneau Shrimper—Walter Satterlee.
* No. 47.  Dutch Fishing Boat—Will H. Drake.

No. 214.   Dutch Girl—Albert E. Sterner.
No. 512.   Afternoon Tea—F. S. Church.

# NORTH GALLERY.

| NO. | SUBJECT. | OWNER OR PRICE. | ARTIST. |
|---|---|---|---|
| 95 | Pansies, | | A. R. Hall. |
| 96 | Fire and Water, | $45.00 | Oliver P. Smith. |
| 97 | Near the Mouth of the Brook, | 40.00 | Wm. L. Sonntag. |
| 98 | An Old House at Hobart, N. Y., | 35.00 | A. Van Cleef Dodgshun. |
| 99 | On a Mill Stream, | 75.00 | Arthur Parton. |
| 100 | A Bit of Scotland, | 100.00 | John A. Frazer. |
| 101 | Outskirts of the Forest, | 500.00 | Edward Moran. |
| 102 | October, | 100.00 | W. Hamilton Gibson. |
| 103 | Birches and Poplars, | Mrs. S. L. Hinckly, | Susan H. Bradley. |
| 104 | A Mountain Stream, | 80.00 | Chas. Warren Eaton. |
| 105 | Old Fish Houses, Nantucket, | 100.00 | Geo. M. Clark. |
| 106 | Summer, | 75.00 | Arthur Parton. |
| 107 | Paris, from Meudon, | 85.00 | J. Wells Champney. |
| 108 | April in the Woods, | 40.00 | Arthur F. Davis. |
| 109 | On the Maas at Dordrecht, | 50.00 | James M. Barnsley. |
| 110 | A Barn-yard Study, | 75.00 | James D. Smillie. |
| 111 | Study, near Riva Garabaldi, Venice, | 200.00 | Henry P. Smith. |
| 112 | Entrance to Buzzard's Bay, | 200.00 | R. Swain Gifford. |
| 113 | Sunshine and Shadow, | 29.00 | Elliott Daingerfield. |
| 114 | Summer Girl, | | Charles S. Reinhart. |
| 115 | The Enchanted Castle, | 75.00 | Charles Mente. |
| 116 | Corn Flowers, | 45.00 | Emma R. Wright. |
| 117 | A Silvery Night, (Illustration.) | 350.00 | Leonard Ochtman. |
| 118 | Smithsonian Institute, Washington, D. C., | 60.00 | James Henry Moser. |
| 119 | From Gloucester Harbor, Mass., | 60.00 | John J. Hammer. |
| 120 | Lorenza, | 50.00 | Miss Margaret Leupp. |
| 121 | In Scented Summer, | Jas. Spooner, Esq., | John A. Frazer. |

9

# NORTH GALLERY.

| NO. | SUBJECT. | OWNER OR PRICE. | ARTIST. |
|---|---|---|---|
| 122 | A Country Lane, | $25.00 | Bert. G. Phillips. |
| 123 | Close of a Summer Day, | 250.00 | Chas. Mente. |
| 124 | The Fields in October, | 75.00 | Carleton Wiggins. |
| 125 | An Honest Face, | 60.00 | W. H. Shelton. |
| 126 | The Informal Call, | 35.00 | Max. Rateau. |
| 127 | White Peonies, | 75.00 | Louise Bloodgood Field. |
| 128 | Still Life, | 30.00 | E. J. Holgate. |
| 129 | Hackensack Meadows, | 190.00 | C. Harry Eaton. |
| 130 | Carnations, | 20.00 | E. J. Holgate. |
| 131 | Roses, | 65.00 | Amy Cross. |
| 132 | A Misty Day on Monhegan, | 75.00 | Ben Foster. |
| 133 | The Tumbling Waves, | 200.00 | F. K. M. Rehn. |
| 134 | September, | 30.00 | Peter Gowans. |
| 135 | The Favorite Pipe, | 55.00 | Claude Raquet Hirst. |
| 136 | Morning, | 150.00 | Arthur Dowson. |
| 137 | Sundown, | 125.00 | J. Francis Murphy. |
| 138 | Midnight, | 100.00 | J. C. Nicoll. |
| 139 | A Drowsy Old Lady, | 175.00 | Clara T. McChesney. |
| 140 | Moonrise, | 350.00 | C. M. McIlhenny. |
| 141 | A Sea Melody, | 500.00 | Edward Moran. |
| 142 | Nasturtiums, | | L. Steele Kellogg. |
| 143 | A Dutch Canal, | L. F. Roos. | V. B. von Tholen. |
| 144 | The Meadows, Brookhaven, | 100.00 | J. P. Woodward. |
| 145 | September, Isles of Shoals, | 150.00 | Childe Hassam. |
| 146 | At the Bend of the Creek, | 100.00 | Wm. C. Fitler. |
| 147 | A Stormy Day off Montauk, | 200.00 | Edward Moran. |
| 148 | Study, | 125.00 | Eleanor E. Greatorex. |
| 149 | Sunset, | 200.00 | Henry Farrer. |
| 150 | Sketch of Muckross Abbey, | 50.00 | J. Wells Champney. |
| 151 | Sheltered Cot, | 40.00 | Peter Gowans. |

* No. 69.   A Cossack—T. de Thulstrup.

No. 406.  Shed and Stack—H. W. Ranger.

No. 374.  Friends—Clark Crum.

| NO. | SUBJECT. | OWNER OR PRICE. | ARTIST. |
|---|---|---|---|
| 152 | On the Meadows, | $250.00 | I. A. Josephi. |
| 153 | Farm Scene, Holland, | Mr. H. H. Vail, | Will H. Drake. |
| 154 | Flowers from the Dunes, Scheveningen, | 150.00 | Amy Cross. |
| 155 | Dutch Fisher Folk, | Mr. H. H. Vail, | Will H. Drake. |

11

No. 613. Before the Days of Rapid Transit—E. L. Henry.

# EAST GALLERY.

| NO. | SUBJECT. | OWNER OR PRICE. | ARTIST. |
|---|---|---|---|
| 156 | German Dragoon, Officer, | $150.00 | T. de Thulstrup. |
| 157 | Clearing Weather, | 50.00 | Henry Farrer. |
| 158 | Street of David, Jerusalem, | 50.00 | James F. Hind. |
| 159 | Millins' Place, L. I., | 15.00 | Mrs. Susan N. Carter. |
| 160 | Snow-laden, | 75.00 | Walter L., Palmer. |
| 161 | Buzzard's Bay, | 125.00 | William A. Coffin. |
| 162 | Landscape, | 60.00 | Kruseman van Elten. |
| 163 | Winter, | 40.00 | Chas. Eugene Moss. |
| 164 | Music, | 100.00 | Jas. Symington. |
| 165 | Sketch at Tottenville, S. I., | 50.00 | Geo. M. Clark. |
| 166 | A High Ball, | 70.00 | Harry Roseland. |
| 167 | Study of an old Mill, Waterford, | 200.00 | Henry P. Smith. |
| 168 | A Corner of my Studio, | 85.00 | H. G. Plumb |
| 169 | Gipsy Girl, | 30.00 | Wm. H. Lippincott. |
| 170 | Morning Effect, | 80.00 | J. C. Nicoll. |
| 171 | Day after the Storm, Wreckers at Work, | 100.00 | Wm. J. Whittemore. |

No. 425. A Glimpse of the Country—Mrs. J. Francis Murphy.

✳ No. 72. Buying Herring, Coast of Maine—Carleton T. Chapman.

No. 313. "Shine, Five Cents!"—J. G. Brown

# EAST GALLERY.

| NO. | SUBJECT. | OWNER OR PRICE. | ARTIST. |
|---|---|---|---|
| 172 | Morning at the Lake, | $350.00 | Kruseman van Elten. |
| 173 | Study in Memphis, Egypt, | 35.00 | M. De Forest Bolmer. |
| 174 | The Stump Orator, | 60.00 | Robert F. Bloodgood. |
| 175 | Afternoon In-doors, | 35.00 | Jos. Lauber. |
| 176 | Coming from the Store, | 200.00 | E. W. Kemble. |
| 177 | A Rainy Day, | 25.00 | Alfred Kappes. |
| 178 | The Old Road Across the Pasture, | 150.00 | Wm. J. Whittemore. |
| 179 | Morning, Long Island, | 175.00 | Edward Moran. |
| 180 | Gray Day (Glen Cove), | 175.00 | Kruseman van Elten. |
| 181 | "One Cen' Apiece!" | 225.00 | Frederick Dielman. |
| 182 | November Morning after a Storm in Looking West, | 70.00 | C. Harry Eaton. |
| 183 | A Gray Dawn, | 125.00 | J. G. Tyler. |
| 184 | Near Ridgefield, Conn., (Illustration.) | 150.00 | Geo. H. Smillie. |
| 185 | Off Tinker's Island, | 200.00 | M. F. H. de Haas. |
| 186 | The Passaic at Millington, | 120.00 | Geo. H. McCord. |
| 187 | Ducks, November, | 120.00 | Geo. Poggenbeek. |
| 188 | Fisherman, (Illustration.) | 75.00 | Jas. Symington. |
| 189 | A Study, | 50.00 | Matilda Brown. |
| 190 | The Gamekeeper, (Illustration.) | 300.00 | L. C. Earle. |
| 191 | Tokay Grapes, | 35.00 | A. H. Kent. |
| 192 | Catherine Mermet Roses, | 50.00 | Grace V. Pomeroy. |
| 193 | Autumn Evening, | 175.00 | V. B. von Tholen. |
| 194 | The Frozen Brook, | 75.00 | Walter L. Palmer. |
| 195 | Family Cares, | 100.00 | Thos. B. Craig. |
| 196 | "Your Bid, Sir!" | | Léon Moran. |
| 197 | A Lesson, | 180.00 | Alice Hirschberg. |
| 198 | Shepaug Valley from Judea, | 120.00 | W. Hamilton Gibson. |
| 199 | Plaza of the Valede Mosque, | 300.00 | F. Hopkinson Smith. |
| 200 | Roses, | 100.00 | Mrs. E. M. Scott. |

13

| NO. | SUBJECT. | OWNER OR PRICE. | ARTIST. |
|---|---|---|---|
| 201 | Selling Fish on the Beach in Holland, | $130.00 | Will S. Robinson. |
| 202 | Portrait of Miss Minchen Schaus, | | Robert de Curvillon. |
| 203 | The Landing-place, | 115.00 | C. Harry Eaton. |
| 204 | Near the Village, | 150.00 | J. F. Cropsey. |
| 205 | Meadow Stream, Ridgefield, | 45.00 | Geo. H. Smillie. |
| 206 | The Sisters, | 20.00 | N. S. J. Smillie. |
| 207 | The Jersey Meadows, | 75.00 | Granville Perkins. |
| 208 | Apples, | 25.00 | K. W. Sellew. |
| 209 | A Reader, | 25.00 | Percival De Luce. |
| 210 | An Idyl, | 50.00 | Percy Moran. |
| 211 | In the Garden, Minster, England, | 75.00 | Childe Hassam. |
| 212 | On the Moor, | 15.00 | John M. Falconer. |
| 213 | Fallen Dignity, | 35.00 | N. S. J. Smillie. |
| 214 | Dutch Girl, (Illustration.) | 100.00 | Albert E. Sterner. |
| 215 | Nook on the Passaic, | 39.00 | Geo. H. McCord. |
| 216 | Low Tide, Scarboro, | 55.00 | E. M. Bicknell. |
| 217 | The Old Town of Torcello, (Illustration.) | | Thos. Moran. |
| 218 | Girl's Head, | 18.00 | Percival De Luce. |
| 219 | The Spirit of Dreams, | 40.00 | Robert F. Bloodgood. |
| 220 | Canal, Venice, | 100.00 | Frank S. Boggs. |
| 221 | A Girl in Black, | 150.00 | Wm. J. Whittemore. |
| 222 | Departure of the Fishermen, | 35.00 | Chas. C. Curran. |
| 223 | A Musical Pause, | 75.00 | Wm. J. Baer. |
| 224 | An Opening in the Forest, | 75.00 | R. M. Shurtleff. |
| 225 | Midsummer Afternoon, | 50.00 | E. M. Bicknell. |
| 226 | An Evening Melody, | 75.00 | Frank Russell Green. |
| 227 | Haystack, L. I., | 45.00 | Geo. H. Smillie. |

No. 493. Thistle—Le Clothilde Bodine.    No. 498. In the Meadows.—W. Merritt Post.

\* No. 117. A Silvery Night—Leonard Ochtman.

No. 334. If Roses Fade—William T. Smedley.

* No. 217. The Old Town of Torcello—Thos. Moran.

## EAST GALLERY.

| NO. | SUBJECT. | OWNER OR PRICE. | ARTIST. |
|---|---|---|---|
| 228 | Ready for a Ride, | $90.00 | J. Wells Champney. |
| 229 | October, | 40.00 | Peter Gowans. |
| 230 | A Tenement House Sketch, | 50.00 | Harry Beard. |
| 231 | Taking the Swell, (Illustration.) | 200.00 | S. R. Burleigh. |
| 232 | The Waiter Girl, | 25.00 | L. E. Van Gorder. |
| 233 | A Duet, | 125.00 | Léon Moran. |
| 234 | Evening, | 50.00 | Henry Farrer. |
| 235 | Among the Dunes, (Illustration.) | 80.00 | W. H. Shelton. |
| 236 | In Summer, | 30.00 | C. E. Cookman. |
| 237 | On Shinnecock Bay, Southampton, | 100.00 | A. T. Bricher. |
| 238 | Where the Brook Lingers, (Illustration.) | 60.00 | W. Louis Sonntag, Jr. |
| 239 | Scene on the New Jersey Coast, | 50.00 | Granville Perkins. |
| 240 | Rose, (Illustration.) | 150.00 | C. Y. Turner. |
| 241 | From the Mountain-side, | 75.00 | R. M. Shurtleff. |
| 242 | Mermet Roses, | 35.00 | Katharine H. Rice. |
| 243 | Palm Grove, opposite Cairo, | 100.00 | James F. Hind. |
| 244 | Breezy Day, Great South Bay, at Patchogue, | 100.00 | A. T. Bricher. |
| 245 | Sweet Violets, | 45.00 | N. S. J. Smillie. |
| 246 | Two Veterans, | 350.00 | R. F. Zogbaum. |
| 247 | Un Appel, (Illustration.) | 250.00 | Aug. Franzén. |
| 248 | Spring Blossoms, (Illustration.) | 400.00 | Kruseman van Elten. |
| 249 | The Path to the Lake, | 25.00 | F. E. Bartlett. |
| 250 | Cliffs at Jeulettes, | 20.00 | Matilda Brown. |
| 251 | June, | 300.00 | Ross Turner. |
| 252 | The Smile and the Frown, | 150.00 | Charles C. Ward. |

| NO. | SUBJECT. | OWNER OR PRICE. | ARTIST. |
|---|---|---|---|
| 253 | Early Twilight, | $125.00 | J. F. Cropsey. |
| 254 | A Spring Note, | 75.00 | Bruce Crane. |
| 255 | In the Woods, November, | | F. Rondel. |
| 256 | November on the Bronx, | 50.00 | Ben Foster. |
| 257 | Sunlight on the Lake, November, | 30.00 | A. J. Roux. |
| 258 | Study of Wild Violets, | 25.00 | Eleanor Palmer Williams. |
| 259 | Forenoon, | 250.00 | Aug. Franzén. |
| 260 | Nasturtiums, | 75.00 | W. Hamilton Gibson. |
| 261 | Warwick Woodlands, (Illustration.) | 200.00 | J. F. Cropsey. |
| 262 | A Minuet, | 500.00 | J. L. Gerome Ferris. |
| 263 | Feeding the Geese, | 60.00 | Benj. Horning. |
| 264 | Street in Suez, Egypt, | 50.00 | James F. Hind. |
| 265 | Two Strings to Her Bow, | | Léon Moran. |
| 266 | At Milton on the Hudson, | 40.00 | J. B. Bristol. |
| 267 | Among the Wharves at Gloucester, | 35.00 | Adéle Williams. |
| 268 | Brook in August, | 200.00 | Homer F. Emens. |
| 269 | Old Dutch Yacht, | 200.00 | M. F. H. de Haas. |
| 270 | Long Island Shore, Fort Washington, | 175.00 | Kruseman van Elten. |
| 271 | On Kettle Island, Coast of Massachusetts, | 125.00 | Geo. H. Smillie. |
| 272 | In Devonshire, England, | 50.00 | E. Wood Perry, Jr. |
| 273 | Before Dinner, | 100.00 | Albert E. Sterner. |
| 274 | Children of Atlantis, | 100.00 | Richard Newton, Jr. |
| 275 | Winter, | L. S. Stone, | Abigail Brown Tompkins. |
| 276 | "Look, then, into thine heart, and write!" | 150.00 | Alice Hirschberg. |
| 277 | Early Morning in a Harbor, | 50.00 | Carleton T. Chapman. |
| 278 | A Katskill Farm-house, | 75.00 | H. M. Rosenberg. |
| 279 | Market Place, Dieppe, | 250.00 | F. Hopkinson Smith. |
| 280 | On the Marshes, | 100.00 | Henry Farrer. |

No. 82.  A Nantucket Back-Door—Geo. M. Clark.

No. 635.  St. Malo, Brittany—Wm. J. Whittemore.

No. 455   Fifth Avenue—Childe Hassam.

| NO. | SUBJECT. | OWNER OR PRICE. | ARTIST. |
| --- | --- | --- | --- |
| 281 | La Belle Cannadienne, | $150.00 | Charles C. Ward. |
| 282 | Winter Afternoon, | 50.00 | W. S. Macy. |
| 283 | Autumn Foliage, | 125.00 | J. F. Cropsey. |
| 284 | Twilight, | 75.00 | R. M. Shurtleff. |
| 285 | Autumn at Cape Cod, | 40.00 | Henry W. Rice. |
| 286 | The Hopkins Mansion, Great Barrington, Mass., | 50.00 | J. B. Bristol. |
| 287 | The Bubble, | 75.00 | Paul Nimmo Moran. |
| 288 | Late Autumn, | 45.00 | Clothilde Bodine. |
| 289 | St. Augustine's Fish House, | 40.00 | Victor Perard. |
| 290 | Near Rouen, | 15.00 | Carrie Stow Wait. |
| 291 | From Lands of Snow to Lands of Sun, | 100.00 | Robert F. Bloodgood. |
| 292 | Head, | 20.00 | Miss E. A. Morton. |

17

* No. 311. A U. S. Cavalryman—Frederic Remington.

# SOUTH GALLERY.

| NO. | SUBJECT. | OWNER OR PRICE. | ARTIST. |
|---|---|---|---|
| 293 | Cabbage-field, | $20.00 | Chas. C. Curran. |
| 294 | " That All! " | 25.00 | Wm. J. Hays. |
| 295 | The Author of "The County Fair," | Mrs. Charles Barnard, | Wm. Wallace Scott. |
| 296 | Bed-time, | 30.00 | M. L. Stone. |
| 297 | Ivory Miniature, | | Mary C. Pursell. |

✳ No. 247.   Un Appel—Aug. Franƶén.

No. 203.  Spring Blossoms—Kensington and Eaton.
No. 334.  July in Summer—C. Harry Eaton.

# SOUTH GALLERY.

| NO. | SUBJECT. | OWNER OR PRICE. | ARTIST. |
|---|---|---|---|
| 298 | A Pleasant Occupation, | $60.00 | Mrs. J. Francis Murphy |
| 299 | December Sunset, | 80.00 | Chas. Warren Eaton. |
| 300 | The Spires of Gloucester, | 75.00 | James William Pattison. |
| 301 | Noon-day Rest, | 175.00 | Walter Satterlee. |
| 302 | A Good Fortune, (Illustration.) | 300.00 | Francis Day. |
| 303 | Sunset, | 75.00 | Carleton Wiggins. |
| 304 | The End of the Chapter, | 75.00 | Claude Raquet Hirst. |
| 305 | Night Mists, | 80.00 | James Henry Moser. |
| 306 | A Memory of Autumn, | 25.00 | A. Van Cleef Dodgshun. |
| 307 | Color Motif, | 25.00 | J. C. Nicoll. |
| 308 | Holly-berries, | 100.00 | W. J. McCloskey. |
| 309 | Campo Santo Margherita, Venice, | 50.00 | Charles S. Forbes. |
| 310 | A Winter Note, | 150.00 | Bruce Crane. |
| 311 | The Evening Glow, Cape Ann, | 97.00 | M. Rouzee. |
| 312 | A June Garland, | 65.00 | Agnes D. Abbatt. |
| 313 | Summer Snowflakes, | For sale | Hamilton Hamilton. |
| 314 | A U. S. Cavalryman, (Illustration.) | 300.00 | Frederic Remington. |
| 315 | Near the Village, Twilight, | 1000.00 | Henry Farrer. |
| 316 | Listening to the Sea, | 150.00 | J. G. Tyler. |
| 317 | George Washington, Andrew Jackson, Randolph, | | S. Jerome Uhl. |
| 318 | "Shine, Five Cents!" (Illustration.) | 400.00 | J. G. Brown. |
| 319 | "May I Counsel Thee, Sister?" | 600.00 | John A. MacDougall. |
| 320 | The Iridescent Sea, | 150.00 | F. K. M. Rehn. |
| 321 | After the Snow-fall, | 100.00 | W. C. Bauer. |
| 322 | American Beauties, | Miss Halliday, | Katharine H. Rice. |
| 323 | Drifting Fog, | 25.00 | Carleton T. Chapman. |

# SOUTH GALLERY.

| NO. | SUBJECT. | OWNER OR PRICE. | ARTIST. |
|---|---|---|---|
| 324 | Sketch, | $15.00 | Amy Livingston Kellogg. |
| 325 | Two Swans all White as Snow, | 50.00 | Richard Newton, Jr. |
| 326 | Campo Mater Domini, Venice, | 50.00 | Charles S. Forbes. |
| 327 | Chapel Pond Brook, | 75.00 | R. M. Shurtleff. |
| 328 | Glimpse of Peasant Life, | 100.00 | Walter Satterlee. |
| 329 | Memories, | 300.00 | C. Y. Turner. |
| 330 | When Shadows Beckon to Rest, | 275.00 | H. M. Rosenberg. |
| 331 | Early Morning, | 75.00 | Max F. Klepper. |
| 332 | The House in Willows, | 175.00 | H. W. Ranger. |
| 333 | A Chat with the Lime Burner, | 125.00 | W. S. Bucklin. |
| 334 | If Roses Fade, (Illustration.) | 300.00 | William T. Smedley. |
| 335 | Study, | 200.00 | I. A. Josephi. |
| 336 | Studio Interior, | 150.00 | Carleton T. Chapman. |
| 337 | Training the Kitten, | 100.00 | J. Wells Champney. |
| 338 | Phlox, | 80.00 | Percival De Luce. |
| 339 | A Dewy Spring Morning, | 250.00 | John A. Frazer. |
| 340 | In Mischief, (Illustration.) | 50.00 | Chas. C. Curran. |
| 341 | Evening, | 40.00 | Charles Parsons. |
| 342 | Calf in the Meadow, | 120.00 | Geo. Poggenbeek. |
| 343 | A Spring Morning, Venice, | 275.00 | Henry P. Smith. |
| 344 | A Gentleman from Japan, | 150.00 | Madame Constance Roth. |
| 345 | A Meditative Maid, | For sale, | Hamilton Hamilton. |
| 346 | The Mill—A Gray Morning, | 110.00 | H. G. Maratta. |
| 347 | An Ocean Tramp, | 150.00 | Henry B. Snell. |
| 348 | The Meadow Sweet with Hay, | 100.00 | Edward Gay. |
| 349 | The Débutante, | 100.00 | Irving R. Wiles. |

* No. 462.  The Legend of the Lake.—A. M. Turner.

No. 373.   In the World, but not of the World—Alicia B. Beard.
No. 340.   In Mischief—Chas. C. Curran.

| NO. | SUBJECT. | OWNER OR PRICE. | ARTIST. |
|---|---|---|---|
| 350 | "Big Ben," Westminster, | $150.00 | Charles Dixon. |
| 351 | Evening, | 150.00 | Bruce Crane. |
| | (Illustration.) | | |
| 352 | Sunshine and Shadow, | 125.00 | Agnes D. Abbatt. |
| 353 | Farm Life, | 85.00 | Charles Mente. |
| | (Illustration.) | | |
| 354 | The Line Fence, | 125.00 | J. Francis Murphy. |
| 355 | Winter, | 40.00 | Chas. Warren Eaton. |
| 356 | Evening, | 150.00 | D. W. Tryon. |
| 357 | Modesty, | 100.00 | Jas. Symington. |
| 358 | Farm at Dublin, N. H., | 35.00 | Susan H. Bradley. |
| 359 | Eleanor, | 350.00 | Frederick Dielman. |
| | (Illustration.) | | |
| 360 | A Friend in Need, | 175.00 | Clark Crum. |
| 361 | An Afternoon Ramble, | 400.00 | A. H. Wyant. |
| 362 | By the Sea, | 100.00 | Melbourne H. Hardwick. |
| 363 | Between the Showers, | 30.00 | Aug. Franzén. |
| 364 | Mending Nets, | 800.00 | Winslow Homer. |
| | (Illustration.) | | |
| 365 | St. Stephen's by Saltash, Cornwall, England, | 150.00 | Henry B. Snell. |
| | (Illustration.) | | |
| 366 | At Nordhoff, N. J., | 250.00 | C. Harry Eaton. |
| 367 | Morning, | 150.00 | F. K. M. Rehn. |
| 368 | November, | 100.00 | S. P. Rolt Triscott. |
| 369 | Gathering Dead Leaves, | 130.00 | J. S. H. Kever. |
| 370 | Study, | 100.00 | Eleanor E. Greatorex. |
| 371 | After Rain, | 125.00 | J. Francis Murphy. |
| 372 | Moonrise, | 40.00 | Arthur Hoeber. |
| 373 | Under the Old Wall, | 80.00 | B. R. Fitz. |
| 374 | Friends, | 225.00 | Clark Crum. |
| | (Illustration.) | | |
| 375 | Near Naarden, Holland, | 50.00 | James M. Barnsley. |
| 376 | Arrival of the Boats, Katwijk Am Zee, Holland, | 100.00 | Will S. Robinson. |
| | (Illustration.) | | |

| NO. | SUBJECT. | OWNER OR PRICE. | ARTIST. |
|---|---|---|---|
| 377 | An English Village, | $100.00 | Charles Parsons. |
| 378 | In the World, but not of the World, (Illustration.) | 250.00 | Alicia B. Beard. |
| 379 | An Autumn Day, | 150.00 | J. S. H. Kever. |
| 380 | Deer and Landscape, | 50.00 | Phimister Proctor. |
| 381 | A Study, | | H. Revere Johnson. |
| 382 | Misty Moonlight, | 500.00 | J. C. Nicoll. |
| 383 | A Leisure Moment, | Artist, | Leo Bruenn. |
| 384 | The Mid-day Meal, | 100.00 | Walter Satterlee. |
| 385 | Evening, | | Horatio Walker. |
| 386 | A Normandy Landscape, | 150.00 | M. Rouzee. |
| 387 | Autumn, | 175.00 | Leonard Ochtman. |
| 388 | Mussel Gathering, French Coast, | 150.00 | M. Rouzee. |
| 389 | Heifer's Head, | 75.00 | Francis B. Townsend. |
| 390 | In a French Garden, | 100.00 | Will S. Robinson. |
| 391 | Melody, | 100.00 | Francis Day. |
| 392 | On the Sound, | 25.00 | George E. Graves. |
| 393 | Landscape, | 20.00 | E. Fenner. |
| 394 | Indian Summer, (Illustration.) | 300.00 | C. Harry Eaton. |
| 395 | Hôtel de L'Ange, Fribourg, | 250.00 | Charles E. Dana. |
| 396 | Country House, | 150.00 | H. W. Ranger. |
| 397 | Bohemian, | 40.00 | Claude Raquet Hirst. |
| 398 | A Group of Boats, | 60.00 | C. Harry Eaton. |
| 399 | The Return of.Spring, | 400.00 | Arthur Parton. |
| 400 | An Autumn Evening, | 250.00 | Julian Rix. |
| 401 | Grizzly Bear, | 75.00 | Phimister Proctor. |
| 402 | Twilight, | 65.00 | Carleton Wiggins. |
| 403 | The Carpenter, | 65.00 | Clara T. McChesney. |
| 404 | A New York Studio, | 150.00 | Ralph Elmer Clarkson. |
| 405 | The Picture Book, | 85.00 | Orrin S. Parsons. |

* No. 182.  Fisherman—James Symington.

* No. 16.  View in Eastern Pennsylvania—W. L. Sonntag.

No. 507. Teatime Gossip. Peter Moran.

* No. 448. Spring Floods—C. A. Platt.

* No. 39. A Summer Idyl—Jos. Lauber.

# SOUTH GALLERY.

| NO. | SUBJECT. | OWNER OR PRICE. | ARTIST. |
|---|---|---|---|
| 406 | Shed and Stack, (Illustration.) | $175.00 | H. W. Ranger. |
| 407 | The Last of the Day, Mahopac, N. Y., | 250.00 | John A. Frazer. |
| 408 | Through the Meadow, Mahopac, N. Y., | 225.00 | John A. Frazer. |
| 409 | With Thoughts Afar, (Illustration.) | 175.00 | Irving R. Wiles. |
| 410 | A Visit to the Studio, | 125.00 | Stanley Middleton. |
| 411 | Rose leaves when the rose is dead, are heap'd for the beloved's bed, | 50.00 | J. Elder Baker. |
| 412 | The Long and the Short of it, | 375.00 | T. W. Wood. |
| 413 | Through the Ferns, | 115.00 | Walter Satterlee. |
| 414 | Calm of Evening, (Illustration.) | 100.00 | F. K. M. Rehn. |
| 415 | Ghosts of a Camp-fire, | 75.00 | Dan. Beard. |
| 416 | Roadside, Evening, | 75.00 | W. S. Bucklin. |
| 417 | Almost There, | 300.00 | Alfred Fredericks. |
| 418 | A Quiet Corner, | 35.00 | A. Van Cleef Dodgshun. |
| 419 | Chrysanthemums, | 60.00 | Mrs. Chas. Goodyear. |
| 420 | The Moat, | 100.00 | B. R. Fitz. |
| 421 | Fading Day, | 50.00 | Chas. Warren Eaton. |
| 422 | The Morning Gossamer, | 150.00 | W. Hamilton Gibson. |
| 423 | Fisherman Mending His Nets, | 75.00 | Childe Hassam. |
| 424 | Making Friends, | 200.00 | Jos. Lauber. |
| 425 | A Glimpse of Country, (Illustration.) | Miss Sara Hallowell, | Mrs. J. Francis Murphy |
| 426 | A Sketch, | | Charles S. Reinhart. |
| 427 | Girl of the Period, | 65.00 | Stanley Middleton. |
| 428 | The River, | 500.00 | Henry Farrer. |
| 429 | Hazy Morning, | 350.00 | C. M. McIlhenny. |

23

# SOUTH GALLERY.

| NO. | SUBJECT. | OWNER OR PRICE. | ARTIST. |
|---|---|---|---|
| 430 | Interior of Great St. Helen's, London, | $75.00 | J. Wells Champney. |
| 431 | The Pastoral Oracle, | 125.00 | F. Morley Fletcher. |
| 432 | Firelight Fancies, | 35.00 | M. C. W. Reid. |
| 433 | Thistles, (Illustration.) | 45.00 | Clothilde Bodine. |
| 434 | Sketch, | 50.00 | Frank Fowler. |
| 435 | October, | 50.00 | S. A. Brush. |
| 436 | Calm Day on the Thames, | 300.00 | Geo. H. McCord. |
| 437 | Market in Thum, Switzerland, | 350.00 | John J. Redmond. |
| 438 | The New Scholar, | 250.00 | E. L. Henry. |
| 439 | A Day in June, | 100.00 | Edward Gay. |
| 440 | Northampton, Mass., | | W. A. Sharp. |
| 441 | Violets, | 20.00 | Cora Marie Gaskell. |
| 442 | A Lowland Pasture, | 225.00 | R. M. Shurtleff. |
| 443 | Girl in Black, | 300.00 | William F. Smedley. |
| 444 | F. D. Millet's Studio, Broadway, England, | 50.00 | Charles Parsons. |
| 445 | In the Studio, | 150.00 | Rhoda Holmes Nicholls. |
| 446 | An Old Canal at Montague, Mass., | 45.00 | C. Austin Needham. |
| 447 | Chrysanthemums, | 40.00 | Adéle Williams. |
| 448 | Spring Flood, (Illustration.) | 250.00 | C. A. Platt. |
| 449 | Early Notes, | 150.00 | K. M. Hugér. |
| 450 | Apple Blossoms, | 20.00 | Maud Stumm. |
| 451 | "T'was a green and rosy world," | 25.00 | M. N. Nelson. |
| 452 | The Love Token, | 750.00 | Wm. Magrath. |
| 453 | Day Dreams, | 200.00 | P. P. Ryder. |
| 454 | In the Meadows, | 75.00 | Arthur Dawson. |
| 455 | Changing Weather, | 250.00 | A. H. Wyant. |
| 456 | A Rocky Shore, Evening, | 175.00 | F. K. M. Rehn. |

\* No. 376.  Arrival of the Boats, Katwijk Am Zee, Holland—Will S. Robinson.

\* No. 414.  Calm of Evening—F. K. M. Rehn.

* No. 190. The Game-Keeper—L. C. Earle.

* No. 341. Evening—Bruce Crane.

# SOUTH GALLERY.

| NO. | SUBJECT. | OWNER OR PRICE. | ARTIST. |
|---|---|---|---|
| 457 | An Autumn Afternoon, | $50.00 | E. J. Dressler. |
| 458 | September Meadows, | 40.00 | Wm. C. Fitler. |
| 459 | A Canal in Venice, | 150.00 | A. H. Baldwin. |
| 460 | Road to Katwijk, Holland, | Mr. H. H. Vail, | Will H. Drake. |
| 461 | The Cliff Road, | 75.00 | S. P. Rolt Triscott. |
| 462 | The Legend of the Lake, (Illustration.) | 700.00 | A. M. Turner. |
| 463 | In Maine, | 251.00 | S. P. Rolt Triscott. |
| 464 | Old Oak Tree, near Montauk, L. I., | 400.00 | Sam'l Colman. |
| 465 | Concarneau Shrimper, | 200.00 | Walter Satterlee. |
| 466 | Fifth Avenue, (Illustration.) | | Childe Hassam. |
| 467 | Ready for a Cruise, | 150.00 | J. G. Tyler. |
| 468 | Regretful Memories, | 250.00 | Percival De Luce. |
| 469 | Confidences, | 450.00 | William T. Smedley. |
| 470 | Mid-Ocean, | 100.00 | F. K. M. Rehn. |
| 471 | Some Pumpkins, | 75.00 | Clara T. McChesney. |
| 472 | The Dock Yard, Venice, | 275.00 | Henry P. Smith. |
| 473 | Rue St. Trovoso, Venice, | 100.00 | Frank S. Boggs. |

# WEST GALLERY.

| NO. | SUBJECT. | OWNER OR PRICE. | ARTIST. |
|---|---|---|---|
| 474 | A Summer Day, | $125.00 | R. Swain Gifford. |
| 475 | Sunday Morning, | 50.00 | Bryson Burroughs. |
| 476 | Dolomites from St. Ulneck's, Tyrol, | 40.00 | Mrs. Susan N. Carter. |
| 477 | A Summer Sea, near West Manchester, Mass., | 30.00 | Charles Baker. |
| 478 | Morning, White House Conservatory, | 100.00 | James Henry Moser. |
| 479 | The Dovecote, | 75.00 | Frederick W. Freer. |
| 480 | Grugère, Switzerland, | 250.00 | Charles E. Dana. |
| 481 | Gossip, (Illustration.) | 400.00 | Frank Russell Green. |
| 482 | German Field Poppies, | $200.00 | Frieda Voelta Redmond. |
| 483 | The Tax Collector, | 150.00 | E. L. Henry. |
| 484 | The Milk House, | 150.00 | H. M. Rosenberg. |

✱ No. 643.   A Cup of Water—Percival De Luce.

✱ No. 261.   Warwick Woodlands—J. F. Cropsey.

No. 240   Rose—C. Y. Turner

* No. 235. Among the Dunes—W. H. Shelton.
* No. 238. Where the Brook Lingers—W. Louis Sonntag, Jr.
* No. 594. The Morning Greeting—L. E. Van Gorder.

| NO. | SUBJECT. | OWNER OR PRICE. | ARTIST. |
|---|---|---|---|
| 485 | Child's Head, | $75.00 | Henry Ihlefeld. |
| 486 | Daisy Field, | 40.00 | Clothilde Bodine. |
| 487 | Spring, | 100.00 | Alex. Schilling. |
| 488 | Silenced, | 90.00 | Wm. C. Fitler. |

"The wheel of time doth pause nor day nor night,
While stay'd forever is thy whirring flight."

| 489 | Drying Nets, | 100.00 | Will S. Robinson. |
|---|---|---|---|
| 490 | Sketch, | J. Symington, | J. F. Mathews. |
| 491 | A Venetian Dream, | 50.00 | Willis Seaver Adams. |
| 492 | Roses, | 35.00 | Miss Sophie M. Nichols. |
| 493 | Sunny Morning, Equihen, France, | 75.00 | George H. Bogert. |
| 494 | Cove and Cliffs at Santa Barbara, | 400.00 | Sam'l Colman. |
| 495 | A Gloucester Hillside, | 55.00 | Frederic D. Williams. |
| 496 | Landscape, | 50.00 | F. De Haven. |
| 497 | The Old Oven, | 50.00 | Alfred Kappes. |
| 498 | In the Meadows, (Illustration.) | 25.00 | W. Merritt Post. |
| 499 | A Grey Day Anasquan, | 50.00 | H. T. Schladermint. |
| 500 | Showery Day in England, | 35.00 | Geo. H. McCord. |
| 501 | Waiting, | 75.00 | C. R. Grant. |
| 502 | Sketch, | 40.00 | C. R. Parsons. |
| 503 | Holly Hock Garden, | 25.00 | Annie G. Sykes. |
| 504 | On the Passaic, | 75.00 | Geo. H. McCord. |
| 505 | Her Choice, | 80.00 | George E. Graves. |
| 506 | Marcella, | 68.00 | Mrs. E. L. S. Adams. |
| 507 | Tea and Gossip, (Illustration.) | 425.00 | Percy Moran. |
| 508 | Snowing, | 175.00 | W. S. Bucklin. |
| 509 | Farm Scene in Holland, | 30.00 | Will H. Drake. |
| 510 | Still Life, | 20.00 | Miss J. W. Clarke. |
| 511 | Irene, | 30.00 | Carle J. Blenner. |
| 512 | Afternoon Tea, (Illustration.) | Simeon Ford, | F. S. Church. |

# WEST GALLERY.

| NO. | SUBJECT. | OWNER OR PRICE. | ARTIST. |
|---|---|---|---|
| 513 | Picked in an Old Garden, | $60.00 | N. S. J. Smillie. |
| 514 | Summer Roses, | 60.00 | Mrs. E. M. Scott. |
| 515 | Sketch from Nature, Jewett, N. Y., | 45.00 | Geo. H. Smillie. |
| 516 | Why Don't He Come? | 85.00 | C. R. Grant. |
| 517 | Winter Morning, | 100.00 | Abigail Brown Tompkins. |
| 518 | Sweet Peas, | 40.00 | Agnes D. Abbatt. |
| 519 | Near Cape Henlopen, | 50.00 | De Lancey Gill. |
| 520 | On the Housatonic, | 100.00 | W. Hamilton Gibson. |
| 521 | Oyster Sloop, Freeport, L. I., | 100.00 | A. T. Bricher. |
| 522 | Portrait, | Prof. J. W. Burgess. | T. W. Wood. |
| 523 | Wild Roses and Elder Flowers, | 115.00 | Agnes D. Abbatt. |
| 524 | Spring Time, | 40.00 | Edward L. Field. |
| 525 | Popendrecht on the Maas, | 75.00 | Charles Parsons. |
| 526 | Monday, | 75.00 | Horace Bradley. |
| 527 | The Jolly Oysterman, Patchogue, | 100.00 | A. T. Bricher. |
| 528 | On the St. John's, Fla. | 75.00 | Granville Perkins. |
| 529 | The End of the Story, | 200.00 | C. W. Conant. |
| 530 | A Fallow Meadow, | 120.00 | W. Hamilton Gibson. |
| 531 | Roses, | 35.00 | Isabel E. Parkes. |
| 532 | Preparing for the Concert, | 150.00 | Jas. Symington. |
| 533 | Round the Country Door, | 35.00 | A. L. Wyant. |
| 534 | Street in a German Village, | 65.00 | John J. Hammer. |
| 535 | Mosque of the 13th Century, Tlemcen, Province of Oran, Algeria, | 175.00 | R. Swain Gifford. |
| 536 | Sketch, | 30.00 | C. R. Parsons. |
| 537 | Roses, | 25.00 | Bessie Brooks. |
| 538 | A Worker, | 50.00 | James Fagan. |
| 539 | Autumn, | 35.00 | Peter Gowans. |
| 540 | Light and Shade, | 25.00 | L. E. Van Gorder. |

* No. 365 St. Stephen's by Saltach, Cornwall, Eng.—Henry B. Snell.

| NO. | SUBJECT. | OWNER OR PRICE. | ARTIST. |
|---|---|---|---|
| 541 | Head, | $20.00 | V. D. Prentiss Singau. |
| 542 | A Bride, | 50.00 | Anna C. Nowell. |
| 543 | To Matinee, | 60.00 | V. G. Stiepevich. |
| 544 | Foggy Morning, | 25.00 | A. T. Van Laer. |
| 545 | Girl in Black, | 45.00 | Mrs. J. Francis Murphy. |
| 546 | Early May, | 35.00 | Alex. Schilling. |
| 547 | The Battery Stairs, | 25.00 | Bryson Burroughs. |
| 548 | Crysanthemums, | 30.00 | Pauline A. Dohn. |
| 549 | The Advance Guard, | 250.00 | R. F. Zogbaum. |
| 550 | Roses, | 30.00 | E. M. Aspinwall. |
| 551 | Colorado Cañon, | 150.00 | Sam'l Colman. |
| 552 | Rustic Courtship, | 150.00 | E. L. Henry. |
| 553 | The Sea, | 130.00 | Will S. Robinson. |
| 554 | Pond Lilies, | 35.00 | Maud Stumm. |
| 555 | The Pipe of Peace, | 150.00 | Frederick W. Freer. |
| 556 | From a North River Pier, | 50.00 | Neil Mitchell. |
| 557 | Winter, | 40.00 | W. H. Snyder. |
| 558 | Manhattanville, | 20.00 | Homer F. Emens. |
| 559 | Landscape, | 40.00 | Arthur Hoeber. |
| 560 | In the Stable, | 70.00 | W. H. Shelton. |
| 561 | Sketch from Nature; Ridge-field, | 45.00 | Geo. H. Smillie. |
| 562 | Twin Lambs, | 50.00 | J. A. S. Monks. |
| 563 | Jeannette, | 50.00 | Léon Moran. |
| 564 | Low Tide, Maine, | 25.00 | Alfred Kappes. |
| 565 | Monday, a Sketch, | 15.00 | A. L. Wyant. |
| 566 | A Wee Maiden, | 25.00 | Mrs. E. L. S. Adams. |
| 567 | Fish Houses, Maine, | 25.00 | Alfred Kappes. |
| 568 | Egypt vs. America, | 40.00 | L. E. Van Gorder. |
| 569 | The Chrysanthemum Season, | 150.00 | Rhoda Holmes Nicholls. |
| 570 | San Geralemo, Venice, | 100.00 | Andrew F. Bunner. |
| 571 | Morning Isles of Shoals, | 150.00 | Childe Hassam. |

29

| NO. | SUBJECT. | OWNER OR PRICE. | ARTIST. |
|---|---|---|---|
| 572 | Music, | $125.00 | Alice Hirschberg. |
| 573 | Abandonnée, Grugère, Switzerland, | 115.00 | Charles E. Dana. |
| 574 | A Jersey Barn, | 60.00 | Frank F. English. |
| 575 | Plateau Country, West of Utah Desert, | 200.00 | Sam'l Colman. |
| 576 | Landscape, | 35.00 | Arthur Hoeber. |
| 577 | A Busy Day on the Thames, | 100.00 | Charles Dixon. |
| 578 | In the Pasture, | 60.00 | Ben Foster. |
| 579 | Potter's Market on the Quay at Wurtzburg, | 400.00 | Louis C. Tiffany. |
| 580 | Chrysanthemums, | 125.00 | Esther L. Coffin. |
| 581 | Morning, | 40.00 | L. E. Van Gorder. |
| 582 | Potomac Meadows, | 40.00 | De Lancey Gill. |
| 583 | Coming Night, | 60.00 | Ben Foster. |
| 584 | Roses, | 75.00 | Anna C. Nowell. |
| 585 | Contemplation, | 50.00 | Frank Russell Green. |
| 586 | Alicia, | 200.00 | Jas. Symington. |
| 587 | Rising Sun Inn, Lynmouth, Devonshire, | 115.00 | Charles E. Dana. |
| 588 | The Coast of France, near Dieppe, | 150.00 | C. Graham. |
| 589 | A Wharf, Freeport, L. I., | 100.00 | A. T. Bricher. |
| 590 | Blackberry Branch, | 40.00 | Miss R. Elisabeth Arens. |
| 591 | Still Life, | 15.00 | Emma J. Smith. |
| 592 | The Little Mermaid, | 20.00 | Abigail Brown Tompkins. |
| 593 | The Stranded Dredger, | 40.00 | Holmes Smith. |
| 594 | The Morning Greeting, (Illustration.) | 75.00 | L. E. Van Gorder. |
| 595 | The Venetian Lagoon, | 150.00 | Andrew F. Bunner. |
| 596 | Sketch on the Meadows, | 30.00 | Adeline Roy Stimets. |
| 597 | Good Bye, | 150.00 | Henry Ihlefeld. |
| 598 | Fish Houses, Maine, | 25.00 | Alfred Kappes. |
| 599 | East River, near Hell Gate, | 20.00 | J. H. Recknagel, Jr. |

* No. 302.   A Good Fortune—Francis Day.

* No. 231.  Taking the Swell—S. R. Burleigh.
* No. 431.  Gossips—Frank Russell Green.

# WEST GALLERY.

| NO. | SUBJECT. | OWNER OR PRICE. | ARTIST. |
|---|---|---|---|
| 600 | Sunset in Holland, | $30.00 | Will H. Drake. |
| 601 | In the Merry Month of May, | 125.00 | Agnes D. Abbatt. |
| 602 | Eastern Shore of Virginia, | 35.00 | B. E. Perrie. |
| 603 | Thistledown, Isles of Shoals, | 150.00 | Childe Hassam. |
| 604 | Summer Sea, | 125.00 | A. T. Bricher. |
| 605 | Evening near Barnegat Bay, | 50.00 | Neil Mitchel. |
| 606 | Harvest Landscape, | 75.00 | W. H. Holmes. |
| 607 | In for Repairs, | 18.00 | Margaret Atwater. |
| 608 | Watering the Stock, | 150.00 | H. G. Plumb. |
| 609 | Through the Mist, Brittany, | 125.00 | George Wharton Edwards. |
| 610 | Clearing the Field, | 60.00 | Benj. Horning. |
| 611 | Marketing, | 50.00 | Alfred Kappes. |
| 612 | November Day, | 30.00 | Adeline Roy Stimets. |
| 613 | Venice, a sketch, | 30.00 | Robert Rascorich. |
| 614 | A Modern Maiden, | | Maud Humphrey. |
| 615 | Spring, Rothenburg, Bavaria, | 75.00 | Willis Seaver Adams. |
| 616 | A September Pastoral, | 150.00 | W. Hamilton Gibson. |
| 617 | "Behold, a Giant am I!" | 38.00 | Amelia M. Watson. |
| 618 | Before the days of Rapid Transit, | 400.00 | E. L. Henry. |
| | (Illustration.) | | |
| 619 | On the Jersey Shore, | 75.00 | W. H. Holmes. |
| 620 | Plums, | 100.00 | Anna C. Nowell. |
| 621 | Near Long Island City, | 35.00 | James M. Barnsley. |
| 622 | French Coast, | 180.00 | C. A. Platt. |
| 623 | Looking Inland, | 75.00 | Melbourne H. Hardwick. |
| 624 | A Judea Trout Stream, | 125.00 | W. Hamilton Gibson. |
| 625 | Going Home, | 15.00 | John M. Falconer. |
| 626 | Sketch on the Holland Shore, | | Josef Israels. |

31

# WEST GALLERY.

| NO. | SUBJECT. | OWNER OR PRICE. | ARTIST. |
|---|---|---|---|
| 627 | Midwinter, | $125.00 | Geo. H. McCord. |
| 628 | In San Guiseppe, Venice, | 75.00 | Jeanie Lea Southwick. |
| 629 | A Study, | 30.00 | A. H. Kent. |
| 630 | Pansies, | 25.00 | Agnes F. Northrup. |
| 631 | Roses, | 35.00 | Harriet N. Leonard. |
| 632 | Portrait, Mrs. C., | | W. M. Chase. |
| 633 | Autumn's Tints, | 150.00 | W. Hamilton Gibson. |
| 634 | A By-Way in Stony Creek, | 40.00 | Mary E. Hart. |
| 635 | St. Malo, Brittany. (Illustration.) | 60.00 | Wm. J. Whittemore. |
| 636 | Through the Poplars, | 75.00 | H. Bolton Jones. |
| 637 | Off To-Day, | 75.00 | Charles Dixon. |
| 638 | Venice from San Giorgio, | 350.00 | Thos. Moran. |
| 639 | Marblehead Harbor, from the Neck, | 125.00 | Hendricks A. Hallett. |
| 640 | The Genius of the Shore, | 30.00 | B. E. Perrie. |
| 641 | At the League, | 25.00 | Bryson Burroughs. |
| 642 | Old Windmills on the Coast of Virginia, | 60.00 | James D. Smillie. |
| 643 | A Cup of Water, (Illustration.) | 100.00 | Percival De Luce. |
| 644 | The Village from the Bluffs, Kennebunkport, Me., | 100.00 | Prosper L. Senat. |
| 645 | Elizabeth Beach, Fisher's Island, | 50.00 | James F. Hind. |
| 646 | A Bit of Clovelly, Devon, | | Charles Parsons. |
| 647 | Hall of the Ambassadors, Alcazar, Seville, | 25.00 | Miss Alicia M. Keyes. |
| 648 | Smoking Peasant, | 75.00 | George Wharton Edwards. |
| 649 | Glimpse of Van Cortlandt Lake, | 45.00 | Wm. C. Fitler. |
| 650 | Chrysanthemums, | 35.00 | Emily P. Mann. |
| 651 | The Dome of the Rock; The Mosque of Omar, Jerusalem, | 250.00 | Harry Fenn. |

✳ No. 353.  Farm Life—Charles Mente.

✳ No. 409.  With Thoughts Afar—Irving R. Wiles.

WEST GALLERY.

| NO. | SUBJECT. | OWNER OR PRICE. | ARTIST. |
|---|---|---|---|
| 652 | Morning at Far Rockaway, Going Out for Blue Fish, | $100.00 | A. T. Bricher. |
| 653 | Near Giovanni e Paolo, Venice, | 100.00 | Andrew F. Bunner. |
| 654 | Sketch in Venice, | 40.00 | Willis Seaver Adams. |
| 655 | Child's Head, | 75.00 | Henry Ihleteld. |
| 656 | The Mater Dolorosa, | 350.00 | Frederick W. Freer. |
| 657 | Nellie, | 35.00 | Amelia M. Watson. |
| 658 | Some Village Houses, | 75.00 | S. R. Burleigh. |
| 659 | Treasures from Japan, | 40.00 | Isabel E. Parkes. |
| 660 | Poppies, | 25.00 | Maud Stumm. |
| 661 | Roses, | 30.00 | Adéle Williams. |

# AMERICAN WATER COLOR SOCIETY.

## 1891

### RESIDENT MEMBERS.

Abbatt, Agnes D.

Baldwin, A. H.
Beckwith, J. Carroll.
Bricher, A. T.
Bridges, Fidelia.
Brown, J. G.
Bunner, A. F.

Champney, J. W.
Chase, W. M.
Chapman, Carleton T.
Church, F. S.
Crane, Bruce.
Cropsey, J. F.

De Luce, Percival.
De Thulstrup, T.
Dielman, Frederick.
Drake, W. H.

Earle, L. C.
Eaton, C. Harry.

Farrer, Henry.
Fenn, Harry.
Fraser, John A.
Fredericks, Alfred.

Gibson, W. Hamilton.
Gifford, R. Swain.

Hamilton, Hamilton.
Hassam, Childe.
Henry, E. L.

Hind, James F.

Jones, H. Bolton.
Jones, Frank C.

Lippincott, Wm. H.

Maynard, Geo. W.
Mente, Chas.
McIlhenny, C. Morgan.
Moran, Edward.
Moran, Leon.
Moran, Percy.
Moran, Thomas.
Murphy, J. Francis.

Nicoll, J. C.

Parsons, Charles.
Perkins, Granville.
Perry, E. Wood.
Platt, C. A.

Ranger, H. W.
Rehn, F. K. M.
Robbins, H. W.
Robinson, Th.

Satterlee, Walter.
Shirlaw, Walter.
Shurtleff, R. M.
Smedley, W. T.
Smillie, Jas. D.
Smillie, Geo. H.
Smillie, N. S. Jacobs.

34

Smith, F. Hopkinson.
Smith, H. P.
Sonntag, Wm. L.
Symington, James.

Tiffany, Louis C.
Turner, A. M.
Turner, C. Y.

Van Elten, Kruseman.

Walker, Horatio.
Weir, J. Alden.
Weldon, Chas. D.
Whittemore, Wm. J.
Wiggins, Carleton.
Wiles, Irving R.
Wood, Thomas W.
Wyant, A. H.

Zogbaum, Rufus F.

## NON-RESIDENT MEMBERS.

Abbey, Edwin A.
Anderson, A. A.
Anthony, A. V. S.

Blashfield, E. H.
Blum, Robert.
Boughton, Geo. H.

Cabot, E. C.
Clark, Geo. M.
Colman, Samuel.
Cranch, C. P.

De Haas, M. F. H.

Edwards, G. W.

Falconer, John M.
Farrer, T. C.
Freer, Fred. W.

Hart, William.
Hennessy, Wm. J.
Homer, Winslow.
Hovenden, Thos.

Jones, Alfred.

Kappes, Alfred.

Linton, Wm. J.

Magrath, William.
McCord, G. H.
Millet, F. D.
Muhrman, Henry.

Newell, Hugh.

Palmer, Walter L.
Parton, Arthur.
Pranishnikoff, Ivan P.

Reinhart, Charles S.
Richards, W. T.
Rondel, Frederick.

Scott, Wm. Wallace.
Shelton, Geo. F.
Snell, Geo.
Sterner, Albert.

Tryon, D. W.

Van Ingen, Henry.

Ward, Charles C.
Waterman, Marcus.
Weir, Prof. Robt. W.

35

# NAMES AND RESIDENCES OF ARTISTS

## WHOSE WORKS ARE IN THE PRESENT EXHIBITION.

## 1891

THE NUMBERS AFTER THE ADDRESS REFER TO WORKS IN THE PRESENT EXHIBITION.

Abbatt, Agnes D., 337 Fourth Avenue—88, 312, 352, 518, 523, 601.
Adams, Mrs. E. L. S., 4020 Drexel Boulevard, Chicago, Ill.—506,
Adams, Willis Seaver—491, 615, 654.                           [566
Arens, R. Elisabeth, 715 Park Avenue, Baltimore, Md.—590.
Aspinwall, E. M., 129 East 17th Street—550.
Atwater, Margaret, Westfield, Mass.— 607.

Baer, Wm. J., 51 West 10th Street—223.
Baker, Charles—477.
Baker, J. Elder, 58 West 57th Street—411.
Baldwin, A. H., 58 West 57th Street—459.
Barnsley, James M., 145 West 55th Street—109, 375, 621.
Bartlett, F. E., 145 West 55th Street—249.
Bauer, W. C., 124 Orchard Street, Elizabeth, N. J.—321.
Beard, Miss Alicia B., 110 Fifth Avenue—378.
Beard, Dan, 191 Broadway—415.
Beard, Harry—230.
Benham, C. C., 247 West 125th Street—17.
Bicknell, E. M., 2 West 14th Street—216, 225.
Blenner, Carle J., 146 W. 55th Street—511.
Bloodgood, Robert F., 58 East 13th Street—174, 219, 291.
Bodine, Clothilde, 19 West 22d Street—288, 433, 486.

36

Bogert, Geo. H., 152 West 55th Street—13, 493.

Boggs, Frank S., Paris, France—220, 473.

Bolmer, M. De Forest, 51 West 10th Street—173.

Bradley, Horace, 143 East 23d Street—526.

Bradley, Susan H., 1217 Spruce Street, Philadelphia—103, 358.

Breul, Hugo, 12 West Street, Boston—26.

Bricher, A. T., 2 West 14th Street—237, 244, 521, 527, 589, 604, 652.

Bristol, J. B., 52 East 23d Street—266, 286.

Brooks, Bessie, 70 Munroe Street, Chicago, Ill.—537.

Brown, J. G., 51 West 10th Street—59, 318.

Brown, Matilda, 9 East 22d Street—189, 250.

Bruenn, Leo, Rome, Italy—383.

Brush, S. A., North Street, Greenwich, Conn.—435.

Bucklin, W. S., Red Bank, N. J.—6, 333, 416, 508.

Bunner, Andrew F., 146 West 55th Street—570, 595, 653. [231, 658.

Burleigh, S. R., Fleur-de-Lys, Thomas Street, Providence, R. I.—

Burroughs, Bryson, 44 Irving Place, N. Y.—475, 547, 641.


Carter, Mrs. Susan N., 140 East 16th Street—159, 476.

Champney, J. Wells, 337 Fourth Avenue—11, 107, 150, 228, 337.

Chapman, Carleton T., 58 West 57th Street—46, 72, 277, 323, 336.

Chase, W. M., 51 West 10th Street—632.

Church, F. S., 58 East 13th Street—512.

Clark, Geo. M., 42 West Tupper Street, Buffalo—82, 93, 105, 165.

Clarke, Miss J. W., 104 East 23d Street—510.

Clarkson, Ralph Elmer, 58 West 57th Street—404.

Coffin, Esther L., 142 East 18th Street—580.

Coffin, William A., 138 West 55th Street—161.

Colman, Sam'l, 42 East 25th Street—45, 83, 464, 494, 551, 575.

Conant, C. W., 187 Washington Street, Brooklyn, N. Y.—529.

Edwards, George Wharton, Plainfield, N. J.—29, 609, 648.
Emens, Homer F., 68 Bank Street—268, 558.
English, Frank F., 104 N. 6th Street, Philadelphia, Pa.—574.


Fagan, James, 3 East 14th Street—538.
Falconer, John M., 148 Madison Street, Brooklyn—212.
Farrer, Henry, Sunnyside Avenue, Brooklyn—56, 149, 157, 234,
Fenn, Harry, Montclair, N. J.—651.                    [280, 315, 428.
Fenner, E., South Orange, N. J.—393.
Ferris, J. L. Gerome, 1520 Chestnut Street, Phila.—262.
Field, Edward L., 19 East 22d Street—20, 524.
Field, Louise Bloodgood, Phillip Building, Boston—127.
Fitler, Wm. C., 30 East 14th Street—146, 458, 488, 649.
Fitz, B. R., 152 West 55th Street—373, 420.
Fletcher, F. Morley, 841 Madison Avenue—431.
Forbes, Charles S., 51 West 10th Street—309, 326.
Foster, Ben, 8 East 17th Street—132, 256, 578, 583.
Fowler, Frank, University Building—434.
Franzén, Aug., Fifth Avenue and 23d Street—247, 259, 363.
Frazer, John A., 114 West 18th Street—3, 42, 64, 100, 121, 339,
Fredericks, Alfred, 200 West 108th Street—417.         [407, 408.
Freer, Frederick W., Art Institute, Chicago, Ill.—479, 555, 656.


Gaskell, Cora Marie, 143 East 23d Street—441.
Gay, Edward, Mt. Vernon, N. Y.—348, 439.              |633.
Gibson, W. Hamilton—31, 102, 198, 260, 422, 520, 530, 616, 624,
Gifford, R. Swain, 152 West 57th Street—112, 474, 535.
Gill, De Lancey, Washington, D. C.—24, 519, 582.
Goodyear, Mrs. Chas., 58 West 57th Street—419.
Gowans, Peter, 28 East 14th Street—134, 151, 229, 539.

Graham, C., 1193 Broadway—588.
Grant, C. R., 80 Washington Square—501, 516.
Graves, George E., 19 West 22d Street—94, 392, 505.
Greatorex, Eleanor E., Paris—148, 370.
Green, Frank Russell, 1512 Broadway—226, 481, 585.


Hall, A. R., 31 West 18th Street—95.
Hallett, Hendricks A., 42 Court Street, Boston, Mass.—639.
Hamilton, Hamilton, 58 West 57th Street—81, 313, 345.
Hammer, John J., University Building, Washington Square—119,
Hardwick, Melbourne H., 12 West Street, Boston—362, 623. [534.
Hart, Mary E., 337 Fourth Avenue—634.
Hassam, Childe, 95 Fifth Avenue—75, 145, 211, 423, 466, 571, 603.
Hays, Wm. J., 246 West 44th Street—294.
Henry, E. L., 121 East 38th Street—438, 483, 552, 618.
Herter, Albert, 841 Madison Avenue—9, 22.
Hind, James F., 57 Vestry Street—158, 243, 264, 645.        [572.
Hirschberg, Alice, University Building, Washing'n Sq.—197, 276,
Hirst, Claude Raquet, 30 East 14th Street—135, 304, 397.
Hoeber, Arthur, 19 West 22d Street—372, 559, 576.
Holgate, E. J., 58 West 57th Street—57, 128, 130.        [606, 619.
Holmes, W. H., 1444 Stoughton Street, Washington, D. C.—67,
Homer, Winslow, Scarboro', Maine—364.
Horning, Benj., 131 Boulevard Montparnasse, Paris—263, 610.
Hugér, K. M., 18 East 23d Street—449.
Hutchins, J. N., 337 Fourth Avenue—37.
Humphrey, Maud, 5 Greenwood Avenue, Rochester, N. Y.—614.


Ihlefeld, Henry, 330 West 48th Street—485, 597, 655.
Israels, Josef, Holland—626.

41

Parsons, C. R., 140 Nassau Street—502, 536.
Parsons, Orrin S., 52 East 23d Street—405.
Parton, Arthur, 51 West 10th Street—99, 106, 399.
Parton, Henry W., 51 West 10th Street—91.
Pattison, James William, Jacksonville, Ill.—300.
Pauli, Richard, Leonia, N. J.—55.
Perard, Victor, 12 East 15th Street—289.
Perkins, Granville, 3 Union Square—207, 239, 528.
Perrie, B. E., 1615 17th St., Washington, D. C.—602, 640.
Perry, E. Wood, Jr., 51 West 10th Street—272.
Phillips, Bert. G., 9 East 17th Street—122.
Platt, C. A., 3 North Washington Square—448, 622.
Plumb, H. G., 34 Beekman Place—168, 608.
Poggenbeek, Geo., Amsterdam, Holland—187, 342.
Pomeroy, Grace V., 101 Park Avenue—192.
Post, W. Merritt, 11 East 14th Street—498.
Proctor, Phimister, 28 West 23d Street—380, 401.
Pursell, Mary C., 70 West 38th Street—297.


Ranger, H. W., 417 West 23d Street—53, 332, 396, 406.
Rascorich, Robert, Venice—613.
Rateau, Max., Montclair, N. J.—126.
Recknagel, J. H., Jr., 23 Monroe Place, Brooklyn—599.
Redmond, Frieda Voelta, 58 West 57th Street—482.
Redmond, John J., 58 West 57th Street—437.
Rehn, F. K. M., 222 West 23d Street—133, 320, 367, 414, 456, 470.
Reid, M. C. W., 357 West 58th Street—432.                [426.
Reinhart, Charles S., " The Chelsea," 222 West 23d Street—114,
Remington, Frederic, New Rochelle, N. Y.—314.
Rice, Henry W., 9 Harcourt Bldg., Irvington St., Boston—285.

Rice, Katharine H., 152 West 57th Street—242, 322.

Richards, Wm. T., Newport, R. I.—87.

Rix, Julian, 19 East 16th Street—400.

Robinson, Will S., 9 East 17th Street—41, 201, 376, 390, 489, 553.

Rondel, F., 145 West 55th Street—255.

Roseland, Harry, 191 Clinton Street, Brooklyn—166.

Rosenberg, H. M., 19 West 22d Street—278, 330, 484.

Roth, Madame Constance—344.

Roux, A. J., 133 Fifth Avenue—257.

Rouzee, M., 142 West 36th Street—311, 386, 388.

Ryder, P. P., 51 West 10th Street—453.


Satterlee, Walter, 52 East 23d Street—33, 84, 301, 328, 384, 413, 465.

Schilling, Alex., 49 West 22d Street—487, 546.

Schladermint, H. T., 80 Washington Square—499.

Scott, E. M., 142 East 18th Street—200, 514.

Scott, Wm. Wallace, 841 Broadway—295.

Sellew, K. W., 61 East 79th Street—208.

Senat, Prosper L., Art Club, Philadelphia—644.

Sharp, W. A., Cartersville, Ga.—74, 440.

Shelton, W. H., 106 West 55th Street—125, 235, 560.

Shurtleff, R. M., 47 West 22d Street—25, 224, 241, 284, 327, 442.

Singau, V. D. Prentiss, 275 Carroll Street, Brooklyn—541.

Smart, Miss A. M., Paris—80.

Smedley, William T., 222 West 23d Street—52, 334, 443, 469.

Smillie, Geo. H., 337 Fourth Avenue—184, 205, 227, 271, 515, 561.

Smillie, James D., 337 Fourth Avenue—50, 110, 642.

Smillie, N. S. J., 337 Fourth Avenue—206, 213, 245, 513.

Smith, Emma J., 1533 P Street, Washington, D. C.—591.

Smith, F. Hopkinson, 150 East 34th Street—199, 279.

Smith, Henry P., 11 East 14th Street—111, 167, 343, 472.

44

Smith, Holmes, Washington University, St. Louis—593.
Smith, Oliver P., 1177 Bushwick Avenue, Brooklyn—96.
Snell, Henry B., 116 West 41st Street—79, 347, 365.
Snyder, W. H., 226 Halsey Street, Brooklyn—557.
Sonntag, Wm. L., 120 East 22d Street—16, 21, 97.
Sonntag, Wm. Louis, Jr., 120 East 22d Street—238.
Southwick, Jeanie Lea, 6 Home Street, Worcester, Mass.—628.
Sterner, Albert E., 65 Boulevard Arago, Paris—65, 214, 273.
Stiepevich, V. G., 1193 Broadway—543.                    [612.
Stimets, Adelene Roy, 307 Montgomery Street, Jersey City—596,
Stone, M. L., Audubon Park, New York City—58, 296.
Stumm, Maud, 473 Main Street, Orange, N. J.—450, 554, 660. [503.
Sykes, Annie G., Woodburn Avenue, Walnut Hills, Cincinnati, O.
Symington, Jas., 58 West 57th Street—48, 164, 188, 357, 532, 585.


Tiffany, Louis C., 7 East 72d Street—579.
Tompkins, Abigail Brown, Newark, N. J.—275, 517, 592.
Townsend, Francis B., 99 Boylston Street, Boston—389.
Triscott, S. P. Rolt, 3 Winter Street, Boston—368, 461, 463.
Tryon, D. W., 226 West 59th Street—71, 356.
Turner, A. M., University Building—462.
Turner, C. Y., 35 West 14th Street—240, 329.
Turner, Ross, Boston—251.
Tyler, J. G., 579 Broadway—183, 316, 467.


Uhl, S. Jerome, 58 West 57th Street—317.


Van Elten, Kruseman, 51 West 10th Street—162, 172, 180, 248, 270.
Van Gorder, L. E., 42 West 23d Street—232, 540, 568, 581, 594.
Van Laer, A. T., 58 West 57th Street—544.
Von Tholen, V. B., The Hague—143, 193.

www.ingramcontent.com/pod-product-compliance
Lightning Source LLC
Chambersburg PA
CBHW030543270326
41927CB00008B/1494